Grammy's Gourmet

By: Pat Ziegler

ISBN: 978-0-9839674-0-8

FORWARD

There are several people who deserve to be recognized for their part in this book. These individuals did not contribute recipes, but without them, it would not have been completed or read quite as well.

First I want to thank Phil Hoehn for telling me that I needed a challenge in my life when I retired (or retarded). Believe me, this cookbook was an experiment. When I cook, I rarely measure anything and almost always "tweak" the recipe. So I had to make so many of these recipes and measure everything. So – Thanks PHIL.

Secondly, I have to thank my son, Brian. When my computer got the "blue screen of death", Brian spent months with the old hard drive retrieving this collection. There aren't enough words to express my gratitude to him for his efforts.

Next is Jeane Doan. She read through the entire book and made many corrections. Thanks to her you will enjoy "poppy" seed chicken instead of "potty" seed. Imagine how good that would have been. Also, we all wanted to make sure that Pam Elliott was not one year older, as I either can't add or subtract her age with the year 2009. Much appreciation for your efforts Jeane.

Then there was my creative daughter, Becki. She did add recipes, but she also created the cover (front and back). Now if that was not enough, Becki thought up the name for this creation "Grammy's Gourmet". I loved it and hope you do also.

Of course, without Progressive Printing and Mike Padenich, this would have never made it to book form. Mike had to endure a whole weekend with me to get this info ready for him. I had to keep him away from the dogs, cats and pool to work on this and that was a contest of will. Thanks Mike.

Much credit is also given to all the chefs that gave me their treasured recipes to add. I know that I love trying new food and sharing all the ways to produce it. Most of these are my favorite recipes and I get tired of looking all over for the main ingredients. Since I always have people asking how I make something, I have taken care of two problems with one book. As you can see, a lot of people contributed to this effort. Some of them are no longer with us. From the latter group I received more positive instructions than just cooking. I hope with this book, a small part of their gift to me will keep on giving.

ENJOY

PAT ZIEGLER

If you need to contact me about any of the recipes – feel free to "holler".
patziegler1@comcast.net

Contents

Contents

Contents

Contents

Appetizers

Bacon and Cheese Canapés

Pat

1 pound bacon
8 ounces of shredded cheddar cheese
1 cup mayo
1 party loaf rye or pumpernickel

Combine bacon, cheese and mayo

Chill until 1 hour before use
Spread on bread slices

Bake at 350°F for 10 minutes or until cheese melts

Bacon Cheese Ball

Pat

Combine
8 ounce cream cheese
1/4 cup pimentos - drained
1 cup soda crackers
5 slices bacon crumbled

Add
I package dry onion soup mix
2 cups of sour cream

Shape into ball and refrigerate

Bacon Cheese Puffs

Pat

6 pieces of bread
12 slices bacon
1 cup shredded cheddar cheese
Butter

Trim bread and cut into 4 squares each

Butter each square and put bacon in center
Sprinkle with cheese

Roll up and secure with toothpick
Sprinkle with cheese

Bake 20 minutes at 400°F

Bacon Cheese Ring

Ellen Dodd

1 pound bacon
1 large extra sharp cheddar cheese, grated
1 bunch of green onions finely chopped
2 cups of mayo
1 teaspoon cayenne pepper
1/2 cup toasted slivered almonds
Strawberry Preserves to serve
Crackers or French bread slices

Fry bacon until crisp - Drain well & crumble
In medium mixing bowl combine bacon, cheese, onions, mayo, & pepper; mix thoroughly. Place almonds in bottom of an oiled 7 cup ring mold; press cheese mixture into mold.

Refrigerate overnight
Unfold cheese ring onto platter.

Place a small Custard cup filled with strawberry preserves in the center of the ring.

Serve with crackers or French bread slices

I

Bean Dip
Eileen Tucker

32 ounces of refried beans
1 can Campbell bean soup
15 ounces of Brooks hot chili beans
16 ounces of hot salsa
1/4 cup cilantro
1 pound of Webber Farms pulled pork
3 cups of mild cheddar

Mix all ingredients except cheese and bake at 350°F till hot and bubbly.
Top with cheese and return to oven for 5 minutes.

Braunschweiger Loaf
Mom

1 Pound chicken liver
2 packages of green onion dip mix
1 Teaspoon sugar

Mix and roll into a ball and refrigerate.

2 - 3 ounce packages of cream cheese softened
1 Tablespoon milk
1/4 Teaspoon hot pepper sauce

Spread cheese mixture over chicken liver ball.

Serve with crackers

Cheese Ball
Pat

8 ounces cream cheese
3 ounces chipped beef chopped fine
(divided)
Small onion or green onions chopped fine
Dash soy sauce
Dash Worcestershire sauce

Form all ingredients into a ball or place in a dish - put remaining chipped beeg on outside of ball if desired.

Cheese Spread
Becki

5 ounce jar of Kraft Old English Cheese
8 ounce cream cheese
chili powder

Mix softened cream cheese with old English cheese and add chili powder to taste.

Serve with bagels or crackers.

Chicken Jalapeno Dip
Ellen Dodd

1 can of cream of chicken soup
1 large can (12.5 ounce) chunk chicken drained
8 ounces of cream cheese
Jalapenos pepper to taste (appx 2 Tablespoons)

Mix all ingredients and microwave until warm.

Serve with Fritos

Appetizers

Cucumber Sandwiches
Granny Tucker

1/2 package Hidden Valley Ranch
12 ounces of cream cheese
1/2 - 3/4 cup mayo
Sprinkle of dill
Burplassor British cucumber skinned

Skin and mince 1/2 of cucumber and mix with all other ingredients

Butter bread generously
Spread cucumber mixture over butter and then top with thin slice of cucumber

White bread is fine, cut in quarters and remove crust

Glazed Bacon
Pat

1 pound bacon
1 cup brown sugar
1/4 cup of orange juice
2 tablespoons Dijon mustard
Bake bacon 10 minutes at 350°F

Combine sugar, OJ, mustard. Pour 1/2 of this mixture over bacon.
Bake 10 more minutes

Turn bacon over and then pour the remaining mixture over the bacon
Return to oven for 15 minutes longer

Hanky Panks
Ellen Dodd

1 pound sausage
1 pound ground beef

1 teaspoon red pepper
1/2 teaspoon each of oregano, onion flakes, and garlic salt
1 pound Velveeta cheese
1 loaf of party rye

Brown sausage and beef and drain
Add spices and cheese and heat until cheese melts.
Spread on party rye and place on cookie sheet
Bake at 400°F for 10-12 minutes

Hot Ham and Cheese Spread
Pat

8 ounce cream cheese softened
1 cup shredded cheddar cheese
3 slices smoked ham, finely chopped
1/8 teaspoon red cayenne pepper
Crackers
Mix cream cheese, cheddar cheese, ham and pepper until blended.
Spread into 9 inch pie plate

Bake at 350°F for 20-25 minutes or until lightly browned.
Serve warm

Hot Reuben Spread
Ellen Dodd

3 packages of 2.5 ounces of dried corn beef
8 slices of Swiss cheese
8 slices of American cheese
16 ounces of sauerkraut
1 cup mayo

Mix all ingredients together and bake at 350°F for 20 minutes.
Serve with crackers or party rye.

Appetizers

Nacho Dip
Kim Craig

1 pound of ground beef
1 can chili con carne
1/2 pound of Velveeta
1/2 pound Mexican Velveeta
Nacho Chips
Brown Meat
Stir in chili and simmer 5 minutes
Add cheeses and melt

Serve with Nacho Chips

Scallops - Sautee
Pat

4 tablespoons butter
2 cloves of garlic crushed
Sautee scallops for several minutes
on both sides.

Spinach Dip
Pat

1 Box Knorr Vegetable Soup Mix
1 Cup Hellmann's Mayo
1 1/2 cup sour cream
1-2 bunches of green onions
chopped
1 can water chestnuts, drained &
chopped

10 ounce package of frozen spinach

Mix all ingredients and serve with
crackers

Another option is to use a pound loaf
of bread and hollow out the center
and use the extra pieces for dipping

Strawberry Pretzel
Granny Tucker

Crush 2 cups of pretzels
1 stick of butter
3 tablespoons brown sugar
Mix and press into 9 x 13 baking dish
Bake for 15 minutes and then chill

32 ounce cool whip
8 ounces cream cheese
1 cup powdered sugar
Mix and spread over crust & back to
fridge

1 box red Jell-O
1 cup boiling water
1 box frozen strawberries
Put on top of cool whip mixture and
return to fridge to cool and gel

Sun-Dried Tomato Spread
Pat

2 packages (8 ounces each) cream
cheese, softened
2 cups mayo (Hellmann's)
1/4 cup finely chopped onions
4 cloves garlic, minced
1 jar (7 ounces) oil packed sun dried
tomatoes, drained and chopped
2/3 cup chopped sweet red peppers
2 cups shredded mozzarella cheese
2 cups shredded Italian cheese blend
1 cup shredded Parmesan cheese,
divided
Assorted crackers

In a large mixing bowl, combine the
cream cheese, mayo, onion, and
garlic until blended.
Stir in tomatoes and peppers.
Stir in mozzarella, Italian cheese

blend and 2/3 cup of Parmesan
cheese.
Transfer to a greased 13 x 9 inch
baking dish. Sprinkle the remaining
Parmesan cheese on top. Bake
uncovered at 350°F for 18-22
minutes or until edges are bubbly
and lightly browned.
Serve with crackers

Taco Salad
Pat

8 ounce cream cheese
8 ounce French onion dip
Cream together these two for bottom
of 9 x 13 dish
1 pound ground beef
1 package taco seasoning

Prepare according to taco directions
Spread over cream cheese layer
Layer lettuce
Layer tomatoes
Layer cheese
Taco chips

Vegetable Pizza
Pat

2 large cans of crescent rolls
2 packages of 8 ounce cream cheese
2/3 cup of Hellmann's mayo
1 package ranch dressing
Assortments of vegetables
Shredded cheese

Roll out crescent rolls and bake until
golden brown for crust
Mix together cream cheese, mayo
and ranch dressing, spread over rolls
Place assorted veggies on cream

cheese mixture
top with shredded cheese

Warm Bacon Cheese
Pat

8 ounce cream cheese
1 1/2 cup sour cream
2 cups shredded cheddar cheese
1 1/2 teaspoon Worcestershire sauce
1 pound of bacon
1-2 bunches of green onions
Large loaf of sour dough bread (or
pumpernickel)

Scoop a large hole out of the bread,
saving the insides for scooping. Mix
together all the ingredients and put in
the bread. Bake at 325°F for 1 hour

Water Chestnuts Wraparounds
Pat

2 cans of water chestnuts
1 pound of bacon
Barbecue sauce
Brown sugar

Cut bacon slices into thirds and wrap
around water chestnuts. Secure with
toothpick.
Bake at 350°F until crisp
Place water chestnuts into crock-pot
with your choice of BBQ sauce and
add brown sugar to taste
Cook in crock pot for 1 hour on low

Banana Bread

Bev Eiding

2 1/2 cups flour
1 1/4 teaspoon baking powder
1 2/3 cup sugar
1 teaspoon baking soda
1 teaspoon salt

Mix these ingredients together

In blender mix:

2/3 cup vegetable oil
2/3 cup buttermilk
4-5 ripe bananas
2 eggs
Pour this mixture into dry ingredients

Two well greased loaf pans
350°F for 45 minutes

Cheese Bread

Becki

1/4 cup sour cream
1/2 cup mayo
2 cups cheese
1 Tablespoon ranch dressing

Mix together and put on Texas toast and cook according to directions on the Texas toast container.

Corn Bread

"Little" Grammy

3 eggs beaten slightly
2 cups buttermilk
1 teaspoon salt
1 teaspoon baking soda

Mix well
Add
2 cups corn meal
Let stand for 15 minutes

If you have a #10 cast iron skillet put heaping tablespoon of Crisco in it and melt on cook top
(if not cast iron skillet use a baking pan 8x8).

Pour mixture into skillet and put in 450°F preheated oven for 15 minutes

Dressing for Thanksgiving

Grandma Schilling

3 loaves of bread (you choose the kind you like your stuffing made out of)
6 eggs (beaten)
2 teaspoons sage
1 teaspoon celery seed
1 medium size onion chopped fine
1 teaspoon parsley
Salt and pepper to taste
Tear bread apart and put all the above in large bowl.

Combine following ingredients
2 cups boiling water
3 chicken bouillon cubes
1 stick butter
Pour over bread and mix well

Either stuff turkey or place in crock-pot (if using crock-pot I melt another stick of butter and pour in over the top).
Turn the crock-pot on and let it cook while the turkey is cooking (several hours on high).

Pumpkin Bread

Pat

Mix:
3 cups sugar
1 cup vegetable oil
4 eggs - beaten
Add:
1 pound can of pumpkin
Add:
3 1/2 cups flour
2 teaspoons baking soda
2 teaspoons salt
1/2 teaspoon ground cloves
1 teaspoon each of cinnamon,
allspice, and nutmeg
2/3 cup water

Two well greased baking dishes
Preheated 350°F
Bake for 1 hour

Zucchini Bread

Pat

Mix Dry Ingredients
3 cups flour
1 teaspoon salt
1 teaspoon baking soda
3 teaspoons cinnamon
3/4 teaspoon nutmeg
1/4 teaspoon baking powder

Add:
3 teaspoons vanilla
3 eggs beaten
1 cup oil
2 cups sugar
2 cups finely chopped zucchini

Two well greased loaf pans
Preheated 325°F Bake for 1 hour

Candy

Buckeyes
Pat

1/2 to 3/4 cup butter
1 pound powdered sugar
1 1/2 cup peanut butter (choosy choose Jif)
12 ounces of semi sweet chocolate chips
2 tablespoons Crisco

Cream butter, sugar and peanut butter
Roll into balls

Melt: sugar and chocolate chips

Dip balls in chocolate mixture leaving the top uncovered.
Place on cookie sheet covered with wax paper and place in refrigerator until solid

Creamy Chocolate Fudge
Pat

1 cup (16 oz.) semi-sweet chocolate pieces
1 pound of powdered sugar
6 tablespoons milk (room temp)
1 teaspoon vanilla
1/4 teaspoon salt
1/4 cup soft butter
1 cup pecans (optional)

Melt chocolate pieces over low heat.
Combine in mixing bowl: powdered sugar, evaporated milk, vanilla, and salt; stir until smooth.
Add melted chocolate; stir until blended.
Stir in soft butter.

Mix in nuts (if desired).
Spread in buttered 8 inch square pan; chill until firm.

Peanut Brittle
Pam Elliott

1 cup sugar
1/2 cup light corn syrup
1 cup salted peanuts
1 teaspoon butter
1 teaspoon vanilla
1 teaspoon baking soda

In 2 quart glass microwave safe bowl cook sugar and corn syrup on high heat for 4 minutes
Stir in peanuts and microwave 3-5 minutes (do not allow to burn)
Stir in butter and vanilla - microwave 1 minute
Stir in baking soda gently until foamy
Quickly pour onto non-stick cookie sheet, spread thin with bottom of spoon.
Mixture is very HOT - be careful when pouring

Peanut Butter Fudge
Pat

Butter sides of heavy 2 quart saucepan
Combine:
2 Cup sugar
2/3 cup milk
Stir over medium heat till sugar dissolves and mixture boils.
Cook to a soft ball stage (234° or around 5 minutes) stirring constantly.
Remove from heat and quickly add:
1/2 pint jar of marshmallow crème

1 Cup peanut butter (can use chunky)
6 ounces of semi-sweet chocolate
chips
1 Teaspoon vanilla
Pour into buttered 8 x 8 dish
Cut when firm

Toffee

Jane Strasser

Equal parts butter and brown sugar

Heat to medium hard crack with
stirring

Pour onto greased cookie sheet

Top with milk chocolate and chopped
walnuts

Cookies

Chocolate No Bake Cookies
Kim Craig

Boil together for 1 minute
1/2 cup milk
2 cups sugar
1/2 cup butter

Mix in:
2/3 cup peanut butter
3 cups oats
6 teaspoons cocoa
1 teaspoon vanilla

After blended drop on wax paper

Congo Bars
Aunt Flo

2 3/4 cups flour
2 1/2 teaspoons baking powder
1/2 teaspoon salt
Mix together above ingredients

Melt: 2/3 cup butter and add:
2 1/4 cups packed brown sugar
Add flour mixture to sugar mixture.
Top with 1 cup of chopped nuts and
16 ounces of chocolate chips

Bake at 350°F in well greased 9 x 13
dish for 25-30 minutes

Hungarian Cookies
Aunt Flo

2 sticks of butter
1 cup of sugar
2 heaping tablespoons Crisco
4 1/2 cups flour
4 egg yolks
2 teaspoons lemon extract

dash salt
4 ounce sour cream to make stiff
dough

Use softened or melted butter,
mixing the remaining ingredients
Preheat to 350°F
Spoon on cookie sheet and bake for
10 minutes

Logs
Kay Kolb

1 cup butter
2 teaspoons rum flavoring
2 teaspoons vanilla
3/4 cup sugar
1 egg
3 cups flour
1 teaspoon nutmeg
Melt butter and add flavorings and
sugar, then add flour, egg and
nutmeg. Dough will be thick.

Roll the logs in 1/2" x 3"
They will not rise so you can put
them close together on the cookie
sheet
Bake for 15 minutes

Icing
3 Tablespoons butter
1/2 teaspoon vanilla
1 teaspoon rum flavoring
2 1/2 cups powdered sugar
Mix these together and then add
food coloring of choice
Red/green for Xmas
Purple/Yellow for Easter
Red/Blue 4th of July

These are my personal favorite
cookie

Cookies

Oatmeal Cookies
Pat

1 1/4 cups butter
3/4 cup brown sugar
1/2 granulated sugar
1 egg
1 teaspoon vanilla
1 1/2 cups flour
1 teaspoon salt
1 teaspoon cinnamon
1/4 teaspoon nutmeg
3 cups oats
1 cup raisins

Cream together:
Butter, sugars, egg, vanilla

Add:
Flour, spices, oats and raisins

Drop on greased cookie sheet

Bake at 350°F for 8 -10 minutes or until light brown

Peanut Blossoms
Kim Craig

1 3/4 cups flour
1 teaspoon soda
1 teaspoon salt

Mix together
Cream together:
1/2 cup butter
1/2 cup peanut butter

Add: 1/2 cup sugar and 1/2 cup brown sugar

Blend in dry ingredients

Shape into balls

Place on cookie sheet

Bake at 375°F for ten minutes

Place candy kiss on each cookie and bake 2-5 minutes longer

Peanut Butter Cookies
Mom

1 cup brown sugar
1 cup granulated sugar
1 cup butter
1 cup Jif Peanut Butter
2 1/2 cups flour
1/2 teaspoon baking soda
2 eggs
2 teaspoons baking powder
1/2 teaspoon salt

Cream together:
Butter, sugars, and PB

Add:
Flour, soda, powder, salt and eggs

Roll into ball (you might want to get your hands wet with cold water so as not to stick)

Take a fork and press into ball twice as an X (dip fork in water so as not to stick)

Bake at 350°F for 10 minutes or until brown

Cookies

Reese Cookies
Kim Craig

1 cup peanut butter
1 cup sugar
1 egg
Hershey kisses

Mix first 3 ingredients well and roll into small balls

Place on greased cookie sheet

Put candy kiss in center

Bake at 350°F for 5 minutes

Sandwich Cookies
Kay Kolb

3 cups flour
1 teaspoon salt
1 1/2 teaspoons baking soda
1 1/2 cups brown sugar
3/4 cup butter
2 tablespoons water
12 ounces semi-sweet chocolate chips
2 eggs

Melt butter, chocolate, and water. Add sugar

Mix flour, salt, soda

Add dry ingredients along with eggs to chocolate mixture.

Bake at 350°F for 8-10 minutes

Make the cookies small because they are sandwich cookies

Icing
3 cups powdered sugar
1/3 cup butter
1/8 teaspoon salt
1/8 teaspoon rum flavoring
1/4 cup milk

Mix all the above ingredients

When cookies are cool put icing on flat side of cookie and add a top layer to sandwich them

Snowballs
Kim Craig

3/4 cup butter
1 teaspoon vanilla
1 tablespoon water
1 cup chopped pecans
1/8 teaspoon salt
1/2 cup sugar
2 cups flour
6 ounces chocolate chips
Colored sugar

Combine:
Butter, vanilla, water, salt, sugar.

Stir in :
Flour and chocolate chips

Form into 1" balls

Roll in pecans

Bake 30 minutes at 300°F

Roll in colored sugar

Walnut Crescents

Kay Kolb

1 cup butter
1/2 cup powdered sugar
2 teaspoon vanilla
1/2 teaspoon salt
1 cup finely chopped walnuts
1 3/4 cups flour

Cream butter, sugar, vanilla, salt
Stir in nuts and flour
Chill and then shape into crescents

Bake 325°F for 18-20 minutes

Dessert

Apple Cinnamon Bars
Marshann Kinman

Bars
1/2 cup butter
1/2 cup sugar
1/2 cup packed brown sugar
1/2 cup apple butter
2 eggs
1 teaspoon vanilla
1 3/4 cups flour
1/2 teaspoon baking soda
1/2 teaspoon salt
1 cup finely chopped & peeled apple
1 cup cinnamon-flavored baking chips (10 ounce bag)

Glaze
1 cup powdered sugar
2 tablespoons milk

Preheat oven to 350. Spray 13 x 9 pan with cooking spray

In large bowl, beat butter, granulated sugar and brown sugar with electric mixer until light and fluffy. Add apple butter, eggs and vanilla . Beat until blended.

Add flour, baking soda, and salt until blended. Stir in apple and cinnamon chips. Spread into pan.

Bake 28-32 minutes or until edges begin to pull away from sides of pan and top is evenly browned.

Cool in pan for at least one hour.

In small bowl, mix glaze ingredients until thin enough to drizzle. Drizzle over bars

Apple Crisp
Pat

5 to 6 cups sliced and peeled cooking apples (or 2 cans of apples for pies)
1/2 cup of flour
1/2 cup of oats
3/4 cup brown sugar
1 teaspoon cinnamon
1/2 cup of butter

In 8x8 baking dish arrange apples. Combine flour, rolled oats, brown sugar and cinnamon.

Add melted butter to make crumbly.

Sprinkle over top of apples.

Cook uncovered in microwave for 12 minutes or until apples are tender

Apple Pie
Little Grammy

Two pie crusts
2.5 pounds of apples, peeled and sliced
1 - 1.5 cups sugar
1 teaspoon cinnamon
Sprinkle nutmeg
2-3 tablespoons flour
one stick butter

Put pie crust in bottom of pie plate.
Add apples
Mix together sugar, cinnamon, nutmeg and flour and sprinkle over apples
Cut butter into thin slices and arrange over apples

Dessert

Put top crust on pie
Rub pie crust with milk and then sprinkle with sugar.

Bake 350°F for around 1 hour or until golden brown

Apple yellow cake
Pat

1 box yellow cake mix
1 stick butter
melt butter, blend with cake mix and put in the bottom of a 9 x 13 baking dish. Bake at 350°F for 10 minutes

Mix together
1 can apple drained
1/2 cup sugar
1/2 teaspoon cinnamon
8 ounces sour cream
1 eggs

Spoon on top of cake and return to oven for 20 minutes

Arkansas Dump Cake
Granny Tucker

1 stick melted butter
1 egg
mix together in the bottom of 9 x 13 pan
1 yellow cake mix (sprinkle on top of butter/egg)
8 ounce cream cheese
3 cups powdered sugar
2 eggs
Mix these three ingredients and put on top of yellow cake mix

Bake at 350°F for 25-30 minutes

Sprinkle with powdered sugar

Banana Caramel Topping
Pat

1 jar (12 1/4 ounces) caramel ice cream topping
2 tablespoons lemon juice
1/2 teaspoon cinnamon
1/2 teaspoon grated lemon peel
5 medium firm bananas cut into 1/4" slices
1 teaspoon rum extract
Vanilla ice cream

In large saucepan, combine the caramel topping, lemon juice and peel, and cinnamon.
Cook and stir over medium heat until heated through.

Just before serving stir in bananas and extract

Serve over ice cream

Banana Layer Dessert
Granny Tucker

1st layer
Cream together:
2 Cups graham crackers
2/3 cup melted butter

2nd layer
Beat together:
1 cup butter
2 eggs
3 cups powdered sugar
1 teaspoon vanilla

15

3rd layer
Drain a can of pineapple (save juice) and set aside pineapple
Dip 3-4 large bananas in pineapple juice and put sliced bananas on top of second layer

4th layer
Spread pineapple over bananas

5th layer
Top with cool whip, nuts and cherries or small chocolate chips

Banana Split Cake
Pat

1 1/2 cups graham cracker crumbs
1 1/4 cups sugar (divided)
1/2 cup (1 stick) butter melted
2 - 8 ounce packages cream cheese
20 ounce can crushed pineapple-drained
6 medium bananas
2 cups cold milk
2 packages vanilla instant pudding (4 serving size)
2 cups thawed Cool Whip - divided
1 cup chopped pecans

Mix crumbs, 1/4 cup sugar & butter. Press into bottom of foil lined 13 x 9 pan
Freeze 10 minutes.

Beat cream cheese and remaining sugar in bowl with electric mixer. Carefully spread cream cheese mixture over graham cracker crust.

Top with pineapple.
Slice bananas over pineapple.

Pour milk into large bowl and mix with pudding mixes. Beat until well blended.
Stir in 1 cup of cool whip and spread over bananas.
Top with remaining cool whip and pecans.
You can also top with chocolate syrup and strawberries.

Banana Split Sundae
Stacey Pruitt

2 3.4 cup graham cracker crushed
1 cup butter
2 medium bananas
12 ounces cool whip
2 - 8 ounce packages cream cheese
4 cups powdered sugar
1 can crushed pineapple, drained
Cherries
Nuts
Chocolate syrup

Mix melted butter and graham crackers and place in bottom of 9 x 13 pan

Mix softened cream cheese and powdered sugar with mixer. Put on crust

Drained pineapple on cream cheese mixture
Cut up bananas in small slices and put on top of pineapple.

Layer cool whip on top of bananas.
Sprinkle nuts.
Put cherries on top.
Drizzle with chocolate syrup
Refrigerate for 4 hours then serve.

Blueberry Jell-O

Granny Tucker

3 cups blueberries
2 tablespoons butter
1 cup granulated sugar
1 cup water
3 tablespoons corn starch

Boil these ingredients for 2-3 minutes
Reserve 1/4 cup of the juice for later

1 box blackberry jell-O
1 box raspberry jell-O
1 1/2 cups boiling water
1 1/2 cups cold water

Add these ingredients to the
blueberry mixture

Put in large bowl and refrigerate for
several hours

Topping
1 cup sour cream
1/2 cup juice from blueberry mixture
4 Tablespoons sugar
1 teaspoon vanilla

Mix these ingredients and spread
over top of firm blueberry mix. Return
to fridge until firm

Butterscotch Chip Coffee Cake

Suzanne Horn

Cake
1 stick butter
1 cup sugar
2 eggs
1 cup sour cream
1 teaspoon vanilla
2 cups flour

1 teaspoon baking soda
1 teaspoon baking powder
1/2 teaspoon salt

Cream butter, add sugar and mix
until smooth.
Add eggs and beat.
Add sour cream, vanilla and mix.
Gradually add flour, baking soda,
baking powder and salt.
Beat mixture until smooth.
Pour 1/2 the mixture into a greased
13 x 9 baking dish.
Sprinkle 1/2 of the topping over the
mixture.
Then carefully add other 1/2 of cake
mixture then rest of topping

Topping (mix with fork)
1/3 cup brown sugar
1/2 cup sugar
1 teaspoon cinnamon
1 tablespoon butter
3/4 cup butterscotch chips

Bake at 350°F for 35 minutes

Butterscotch Pie

"Little" Grammy

Graham Cracker Crust or Pie Crust
3 eggs separated
2 1/4 cups milk
1 1/2 cups dark brown sugar
1/4 teaspoon salt
6 tablespoons flour
4 tablespoons butter
1 teaspoon vanilla
6 tablespoons granulated sugar

Combine egg yolks with sugars and
flour and salt mixture with 1/4 cup
milk.

Cook the above with butter and rest of milk in double boiler for 15 minutes until smooth.
Cool slightly and add vanilla.

Use egg whites for meringue

Caramel Cheesecake Bars
Pat

1 1/2 cups crushed vanilla wafers
1 tablespoon vanilla
1/4 cup melted butter
4 eggs
4 packages 8 ounce cream cheese - softened
24 squares caramel
1 cup sugar
1 tablespoon water
1 cup sour cream
1 cup chopped pecans
3 tablespoons flour
3 squares semi sweet chocolate

Heat oven to 325°F.
Line 9 x 13 baking sheet with foil, with ends of foil extending over sides of pan.

Remove 1/2 of pecans; set aside.
Mix wafer crumbs and pecan pieces with butter.
Press firmly onto bottom of prepared pan.
Refrigerate until ready to use.

Beat cream cheese and sugar in large bowl with electric mixer on medium speed until well blended.
Add sour cream, flour and vanilla; mix well.
Add eggs, one at a time, mixing on low speed after each addition until well blended.
Pour over crust.

Bake 45 minutes or until center is almost set.

Cool completely.

Place caramels in microwave on high for 1 minute or until completely melted when stirred.
Pour over cheese cake and top with reserved pecans.
Melt chocolate as directed on package.
Drizzle over cheesecake.

Refrigerate at least 4 hours.
Use handles to remove cheesecake from pan before cutting into pieces to serve.

Refrigerate leftovers.

Caramel Icing
Mom

2 cups brown sugar
1 tablespoon Crisco
1 tablespoon corn syrup (light or dark and if you don't have either of those honey will work fine)
1/2 cup milk
Boil these ingredients until in a "soft ball" stage (about 5 minutes).

1/3 cup Crisco oil
2 1/2 cups powdered sugar
4 tablespoons milk
1 teaspoon vanilla
Mix these until smooth

Pour hot mixture into mixing bowl with powdered sugar mix. Mix well and let semi cool before pouring on cake.

I usually make a spice cake per package directions and use this recipe as the topping

---

Caramel Pie

Pat

2 cans Eagle Brand milk (regular) Boil in stock pot for 3 hours. Use a tall pot as the water will boil down. Do not open cans.

One large graham cracker crust (either store bought or homemade) 1 can of drained pineapple

Put pineapple in the bottom of the graham cracker crust and put the caramelized Eagle Brand milk on top. Finish with cool whip or Reddy Whip.

O'Charley's does a variation of this recipe. They put nuts and chocolate chips on top of the Reddy Whip.

Cheese Streusel Coffee Cake

Pat

One package yellow cake mix, divided (set aside 1/4 cup)
1 package active dry yeast
1 cup flour
2 eggs

Cheese filling:
2-8 ounce cream cheese

2 eggs
1/4 cup sugar
1 tablespoon flour
1 tablespoon sugar

Topping:
1Tablespoon butter
Remaining cake mix

Glaze:
1 cup powdered sugar
1 tablespoon white corn syrup or honey
1 tablespoon water

Combine first 4 ingredients and put in greased 9 x 13 baking dish

Blend the cheese filling and drop onto cake mixture covering evenly.

Mix topping and put on top of cheese mixture

Bake at 350°F 40-45 minutes

Mix glaze and drizzle over warm cake

Cherry Cream Cheese Dessert

Pat

3/4 cup graham cracker crumbs
2 Tablespoons sugar
2 Tablespoons butter; melted

Filling
8 ounce package cream cheese
14 ounce can sweetened condensed milk (Eagle Brand - regular)
1/3 cup lemon juice
1 Teaspoon vanilla

21 ounce can cherry pie filling

Combine cracker crumbs, sugar and butter
Divide among eight dessert dishes (about 4 rounded teaspoons)

In small mixing bowl, beat cream cheese until smooth
Add milk until blended
Beat in lemon and vanilla
Spoon about 1/4 cup each into each dish.

Top with pie filling (about 1/4 cup each)

Cherry Pie
Pat

Prepare pie crusts

Put 2.5 pounds of tart red cherries in pie plate

Combine:
2 cups sugar
1/3 cup flour
dash salt
Pour over cherries

1/2 stick of butter, cut and place on top of sugar mixture.

Put on top crust.

Bake at 400°F for 15 minutes

Reduce heat and bake at 350°F for 45-50 minutes or until crust is golden brown

Chocolate Chip Cheese Ball
Becki

8 ounce cream cheese
1 stick butter
1/4 teaspoon vanilla
Beat until fluffy
2 tablespoons brown sugar
3/4 cup 10x sugar
3/4 cup mini chocolate chips
Mix in with cream cheese mixture

Serve with graham cracker sticks.

Chocolate Éclairs
Holly Schilling

1 large vanilla pudding mix
Mix as directed on box except decrease milk by 2/3 cup and add:
1 cup sour cream
8 ounce cool whip

Layer:
Whole graham crackers on the bottom of an 8 x13 dish and then top with 1/2 pudding mix, layer graham crackers, rest of pudding mix, and another layer of graham crackers

Icing
1 cup sugar
1 stick butter
1/2 cup evaporated milk
Bring to a boil and boil for 2 minutes
Add:
1/2 cup chocolate chips
1/2 teaspoon vanilla
Pour over graham crackers

Refrigerate for a couple of hours

Chocolate Mug Cake

Carol Flanigan

4 Tablespoons flour
4 Tablespoons sugar
2 Tablespoons cocoa
1 egg
3 Tablespoons milk
3 Tablespoons oil
3 Tablespoons chocolate chips
Small splash of vanilla
1 large coffee mug

Add dry ingredients to mug and mix well
Add egg and mix thoroughly
Pour in milk and oil, mix well
Add chocolate chips and vanilla, mix well

Put your mug in the microwave and cook for 3 minutes at 1000 watts
The cake will rise over the top of the mug, don't be alarmed.
Allow to cool a little - eat

This can serve 2 if you want to feel slightly more virtuous.
And why is this the most dangerous cake recipe in the world?? Because now we are all only 5 minutes away from chocolate cake at any time of the day or night!!

Chocolate Triple Pie

Pat

1 Tablespoon granulated gelatin (unflavored)
2/3 cup sugar
1/4 Teaspoon salt
1 cup milk
3 egg yolks, beaten

3 squares Hershey's Baking Chocolate
1 Teaspoon vanilla
3 egg whites beaten
1/4 Teaspoon cream of tartar
1/4 cupful granulated sugar
1 cup cool whip
9 inch baked pie shell

Mix together gelatin, 2/3 cup sugar and salt in a saucepan, blend in the milk and egg yolks; add baking chocolate.
Heat slowly, stirring constantly, over medium heat until chocolate is melted and mixture thickens slightly.
Pour into a large bowl and add vanilla, stir until smooth and blended.
Cool completely

Beat the egg whites with cream of tartar until foamy in a small bowl.
Gradually add the 1/4 cup of sugar and beat until the meringue stands in thick peaks.

Beat the cooled chocolate mixture until smooth, then fold in the meringue and then fold in half the cool whip.

Pour into baked pie shell.
Chill several hours or until firm enough to cut.
Garnish with remaining cool whip.

Cobbler (any fruit)

Pat

Melt 1 stick of butter in bottom of deep dish pie plate
Add 29 ounce can of fruit - juice and all (peaches are a good one to start with)

Dessert

Mix:
1 cup self rising flour
1 cup sugar
1 egg

Spread on fruit

Bake at 350°F for 35-45 minutes or until brown

Creamed Fill Cherry Pie (no bake)
Pat

Pie crust of your choice (I usually use graham cracker)

1 can Eagle Brand milk (regular)
1/3 cup lemon juice
1 teaspoon vanilla
1/2 teaspoon almond extract
1/2 cup cool whip

Mix all the above ingredients together and put in pie crust.

Top with cherry pie filling.
Put in fridge a couple hours to set

Daiquiri Pie
Pat

Graham Cracker Crust

8 ounce cream cheese
1 can Eagle Brand milk (regular)
6 ounces can frozen limeade concentrate
1/3 cup light rum
green food coloring
1 cup cool whip

Mix all together and put in fridge for several hours

Death by Chocolate
Suzanne Horn

1 Box Brownie Mix
1/2 - 3/4 cup kahlua
2 packages instant chocolate mousse
16 ounce container of cool whip
6 Heath bar crushed or bag of crushed Heath

Follow recipe for cake like brownies.

Bake in 9x9 pan according to direction on the box. Cool for 1 hour.

Make mousse according to directions on the box. Refrigerate for 1-2 hours.

Poke holes in brownies with fork.
Pour Kahlua over top of brownies.

Break up brownies into pieces.
In a clear bowl, layer 1/2 brownie pieces, 1/2 mousse, 1/2 cool whip and 1/3 of Heath pieces.

Continue with additional layer.
Add additional Heath pieces to top.

Éclair Cake
Holly Schilling

1 box graham crackers
2 small packages vanilla pudding
3 cups milk
8 ounce cool whip
1 can dark chocolate icing

Mix pudding, milk, cool whip
Layer in 9 x 13 dish crackers,
pudding mixture, crackers, pudding
mixture, crackers
Icing top of crackers and refrigerate
for 8 hours

Graham Cracker Crust

Pat

1 1/2 cups Graham cracker crumbs
1/2 cup butter
1/3 cup 10x sugar

Melt butter, add graham crackers
and sugar, press in bottom of
whatever pan you are using.

Hershey Almond Pie

Pat

Graham Cracker Crust

19 large Marshmallows
6 small Hershey almond bars
1 cup milk
1/2 pint whipping cream

Mix first three ingredients over low
heat until all melted.

Put in fridge and cool until firm

Whip cream and fold in chocolate
mixture
Pour into crust
Can be topped with whipped cream
or cool whip

Home Made Ice Cream

Aunt Freda

6 eggs separated (whites in fridge)
beat yellow (longer better - I usually
do about 1/2 hour)
Then add 2 cups sugar slowly
1 large package vanilla pudding mix
3 tablespoons vanilla
1/2 bowl milk (vitamin D)

After the yellows are done beating
turn the mixer down to prevent
splatter.

Pour into freezer

Beat cold egg whites until stiff
Pour into freezer

Pour milk to full line in freezer

Put in freezer and add plenty of ice
and rock salt to start and then check
to add more ice and salt as needed.
The more salt you use the faster it
will freeze.

Lemon Pie - Effortlessly

Pat

14 ounce can Eagle Brand
2 egg yolks
3/4 cup lemon juice
1 graham cracker crust
In a large bowl, whisk together
condensed mild, egg yolks, and
lemon juice.
Pour in pie crust.
Bake at 350°F for 7 minute or until
the center is set. Remove from the
oven and let cool for 20 minutes
Cover and refrigerate for 1 hour.

New York Style Cheese Cake
Pat

Graham Cracker Crust

3 packages 8 ounce cream cheese
4 eggs
1 cup sugar
1 teaspoon vanilla
1 pint sour cream

Beat until smooth (except sour cream)
Note: the longer you beat this mixture the lighter and fluffier the cake will be. I actually let it beat for 1/2 hour).

Pour batter in spring form pan
Bake at 350°F for 50 minutes

Spread sour cream on top
Bake additional 5 minutes
Cool overnight

Pay Day Bars
Suzanne Horn

Base
1 Box yellow cake mix
1 Egg
10 2/3 tablespoons butter
2 cups mini marshmallows

Mix all ingredients (except marshmallows) together. Press into a jelly roll pan and bake at 350°F for 12 minutes.
On top of base add marshmallows and bake for 5 more minutes

Topping

1 bag peanut butter chips
2 tablespoons butter
2/3 cup corn syrup
2 cups crispy rice cereal
2 cups salted peanuts

Melt chips, butter and syrup in a saucepan. Add cereal and peanuts.
Pour over base.
Cool.
Cut into squares

Peanut Butter Pie
Pat

Crust:
1/3 cup of butter
6 ounces of chocolate chips
2 1/2 cups of Rice Krispies

Melt butter and chocolate until smooth, add Rice Krispies and put in bottom of pie crust coated with Pam (You can make an Oreo crust according to package directions).
Put in fridge to firm up

Filling
8 ounce cream cheese
14 ounce Eagle Brand milk
3/4 cup Jif Peanut Butter
3 Tablespoons lemon juice
1 teaspoon vanilla
1 cup cool whip

Mix all of these ingredients in mixer until well blended.
Pour over pie crust

Drizzle with chocolate syrup

Dessert

Pecan Pie

Pat

Pie Crust
1 cup light corn syrup
1 cup dark brown sugar
3 eggs slightly beaten
1/3 cup melted butter
1/2 teaspoon salt
1 teaspoon vanilla
1 heaping cup pecans

Combine:
Corn syrup, sugar, eggs, butter, salt,
& vanilla
Mix well
Pour into pie crust
Sprinkle with pecan halves
350°F for 45-50 minutes

Pineapple Nut Cake

Pam Elliott

2 cups flour
2 cups sugar
2 eggs
2 Teaspoons baking soda
20 ounce can crushed pineapple
1/2 cup chopped nuts

Combine and put in greased 9 x 13
pan and bake at 350°F for 35-45
Minutes

Cream Cheese Frosting
2 cups 10x sugar
1 stick butter
1/2 Tablespoon vanilla
8 ounces cream cheese
Mix with electric mixer
Spread on cooled cake

Pineapple Pretzel Dessert

Katie Noppert

16 ounce cool whip
16 ounce cream cheese
1 cup sugar
2 15 ounce cans of crushed
pineapple (WELL drained)
Cream together and refrigerate

2 cups crushed pretzels
1 stick butter
1/2 cup sugar
Mix together
Pour on cookie sheet

Bake at 400°F for 7-9 minutes
Set aside to cool
Store pretzel mixtures in baggie or
other plastic container.

Put pineapple mixture in dessert cup
and just before serving sprinkle
pretzel mixture on top

Pumpkin Cheesecake

Pat

Crust
3/4 cups chopped pecans, toasted
32 gingersnap cookies
3 tablespoons brown sugar
6 tablespoons melted butter

Filling
3 8 ounce packages cream cheese
1 cup brown sugar
1 1/2 cups canned pumpkin
1/2 cup heavy whipping cream
1/4 cup maple syrup
3 teaspoons vanilla
3 teaspoons ground cinnamon
1/2 teaspoon ground ginger

1/4 teaspoon ground cloves
4 eggs, lightly beaten

Place a greased 9" spring form pan on a double thickness of heavy-duty foil, securely wrap foil around pan.
Place pecans in a food processor, cover and process until ground.
Add gingersnaps, brown sugar and butter, cover and pulse until blended.
Press onto the bottom and 2" up sides of prepared pan, set aside.

In a large mixing bowl, beat cream cheese and brown sugar until smooth.
Beat in the pumpkin, cream, syrup, vanilla, and spices. Add eggs; beat on low speed just until combined.
Pour into crust.
Place spring form pan in a large baking pan, add 1 in of hot water to larger pan.

Bake at 325°F for 60-70 minutes or until center is just set and top appears dull.
Remove pan from water bath.
Cool on wire rack for 10 minutes.
Carefully run a knife around edge of pan to loosen, cool 1 hour longer.
Chill overnight.

Remove sides of pan.

Quick Cherry Crunch
Pat

Butter a 8" square pan
2 cups drained canned red pie cherries
1 cup flour
1/2 cup cherry juice (reserved when draining cherries)
1 cup quick cooking oatmeal
1/4 teaspoon baking powder
1 1/2 tablespoons quick cooking tapioca
1/4 teaspoon salt
1/2 cup melted butter
1/4 teaspoon baking soda
1 cup packed brown sugar

Mix cherry juice and tapioca and let stand for 15 minutes
Mix melted butter with brown sugar, flour, oatmeal, baking powder, salt and baking soda.
Put half of the mixture in pan.
Scatter drained cherries over the mixture and then add the juice/tapioca mixture.
Top with remaining pastry mixture.

Bake at 350°F for 30-35 minutes

Serve plain or with ice cream

Raspberry White Chocolate Bars
Suzanne Horn

1 1/2 cups sugar
1 1/2 cups butter, softened
1 tcaspoon salt
2 teaspoons vanilla
4 cups all purpose flour
2 eggs
18 ounce jar red raspberry preserves
1 cup vanilla milk chips
Heat oven to 350°F
Combine sugar, butter, salt and vanilla in large mixer bowl. Beat at medium speed, scraping bowl often, until well mixed (1 or 2 minutes).
Reduce speed to low. Beat, adding flour 1 cup at a time and scraping

bowl often, until mixture is crumbly (1 or 2 minutes).
Remove 1 cup crumb mixture, set aside.

Add eggs to remaining crumb mixture in bowl; beat until mixture forms a dough (1 or 2 minutes). Press dough evenly into ungreased 13 x 9 inch baking pan. Bake for 30 minutes or until lightly brown.

Spread preserves over hot, partially baked bars. Sprinkle vanilla milk chips over preserves.
Sprinkle with reserved crumb mixture.

Continue baking for 20 to 25 minutes or until topping is lightly browned.

Cool completely. Cut into bars

Shortcake

Mom

2 cups flour
2 teaspoons baking powder
1 cup of sugar
1 egg
1/4 teaspoon salt
4 tablespoons butter
3/4 cup milk
1 teaspoon vanilla

Cream together sugar and butter
Mix flour, baking powder, salt
Add dry ingredients to sugar butter mix along with eggs, vanilla and milk

Place in well greased 9 x 13 baking pan and bake at 350°F for approx 50 minutes.

So Good Cake

Granny Tucker

1 box chocolate cake mix
1 can cherry pie filling
1 teaspoon almond extract
Mix and bake at 350 for 20-30 minutes

Icing
1/3 cup milk
1 cup 10x sugar
6 ounces of chocolate chips
Heat until smooth
Spread on cake

Texas Lime Pie

Pat

Graham Cracker Crust

3 cans Eagle Brand Milk
5 egg yolks
2 cups lime juice

Beat milk, egg yolks, and lime juice for 2 minutes on low.
Pour into pie crust

Bake at 350°F for 18-22 minutes
Cool for 1 hour
Chill overnight

Bravo's Bodacious Burger Stew

Pat Ziegler

1 pound ground beef or turkey
1/2 pound millet
1/2 pound spinach, chopped
1/2 pound carrots, chopped
2 cloves garlic, chopped
2 tablespoons kelp powder
4 to 6 cups spring water

Combine all ingredients in a stainless steel pot with enough water to cover. Bring to a boil, then lower heat and simmer for 30 minutes.
Blend all ingredients into a puree. Store in meal size containers and use within 3 to 4 days or freeze.

Cornmeal

Pat Ziegler

I personally don't think dogs need cornmeal (and certainly not cats). When I cooked for the dogs, I would substitute rolled oats for the cornmeal. However, I now feed my dogs raw food. If interested the rule of thumb is 2% or 3% of their body weigh. Make sure they get some green tripe for there veggies. I also give my dogs vitamins.

Dog Biscuits Deluxe

Pat Ziegler

2 cups whole wheat flour
1/2 cup soy flour
1/4 cup cornmeal
1/2 cup sunflower or pumpkin seeds
1 or 2 cloves garlic, minced
2 tablespoons butter, melted

1 tablespoon brewer's yeast (optional)
1/4 cup unsulfured molasses
1 teaspoon salt
2 eggs mixed with 1/4 cup milk

Mix flours, cornmeal and seeds together. Add garlic and yeast (if desired).
Combine the butter, molasses, salt and egg mixture; set a side a tablespoon of this liquid mixture and combine the rest with dry ingredients.
Add more milk, if necessary, to make a firm dough. Knead together for a few minutes and let the dough rest for 1/2 hour +/-. Roll out to 1/2" thick. Cut into desired shape and brush with remaining egg mixture.
Bake at 350°F for 30 minutes or until lightly toasted.
Biscuits will keep longer if you use oil instead of butter.
20% protein
18% fat
57% carbs

Dog or Cat Crunchies

Pat Ziegler

1 pound chicken necks and gizzards or other poultry, ground
16 ounces of mackerel chopped
2 cups full fat soy flour
1 cup wheat germ
1 cup powdered skim milk
1 cup cornmeal (dry)
2 cups whole wheat flour
1 cup rye flour (or another cup of whole wheat)
1/2 teaspoon salt or 3 tablespoons kelp

4 tablespoons vegetable oil (half of can of meat drippings, or butter)
3 cloves garlic, minced
1 quart water
1/2 cup brewer's yeast

Mix all ingredients except yeast and knead into firm dough.
Roll out on a cookie sheet about 1/4 to 1/2 inch thick. Divide into strips.
Bake at 350°F for 30-45 minutes.
Cool and break into bite size chunks.
Sprinkle with yeast and store in airtight containers.

Refrigerate whatever will not be eaten within 3 days.

Liver Brownies

Pat Ziegler

6 eggs
1/3 cup vegetable oil
1 or 2 cloves garlic
2 pounds raw liver
3 cups whole wheat flour
1 cup corn meal
1 cup rolled oats
1 tablespoon yeast
1/2 cup (enough to make a batter)
Beat eggs and oil.
Add garlic
Process liver to a paste in food processor. Add to egg mixture.
Add dry ingredients to the liver mixture, plus enough water to be able to stir well. You want a thick batter.
Spread batter in a greased 17 x 11 jelly roll pan.
Bake at 350°F for 35-45 minutes until nicely browned and firm to touch.
Cool completely.

Cut into bite size pieces.
Refrigerate or freeze.
Use refrigerated brownie with 4 - 5 days.
This treat is very enticing because of the high liver content. It is, however, high in vitamin A, which comes primarily from liver. So use this as an occasional treat, NOT for daily use.

Satin Balls

Sara Eiding Kassow

10 pounds hamburger
1 box Total
1 box oatmeal
1 jar wheat germ
1 1/4 cup oil
1 1/4 cup unsulfured molasses
10 eggs
10 envelopes plain gelatin

Mix all together and form "meatballs" and freeze.
Use as needed.
This is for canine weight gain

Spot's Chicken Stew

Pat Ziegler

2 1/2 pounds whole chicken or turkey (bones, organs, skin and all)
1 cup green peas
1 cup chopped carrots
1/2 cup chopped sweet potatoes
1/2 cup chopped zucchini
1/2 cup chopped yellow squash
1/2 cup copped green beans
1/2 cup chopped celery
1 tablespoon kelp powder
1 tablespoon rosemary
11-16 cups spring water

FOR DOGS ONLY: Add 8 ounces whole barley and 7 ounces rolled oats, and adjust the water content to a total of 16 cups or enough to cover ingredients. (not for cats).

Combine all ingredients in a 10 quart stockpot (stainless steel, please) with enough water to cover. Bring to a boil, then turn down heat as low as possible and simmer for 2 hours. Remove from the heat, let cool, and de-bone the chicken (cooked bones are not good). With an electric hand mixer or food processor (using small batches), blend all ingredients into puree. Store in meal size portions.

Dog's Weigh Portion	Total Daily
Up to 10 pounds	1 to 1 1/2 cups
11 to 20 pounds	2 to 3 cups
21 to 40 pounds	4 cups

for each additional 20 pounds, add 2 cups

Sprinkle with yeast if your dog is fond of it.
This dog biscuit is good for occasional treats or rewards, but to low in protein and other nutrients for regular chow.
15% protein
28% fat
56% carbs

Wheat or Rye Crisps for Dogs
Pat Ziegler

1 cup whole wheat or rye flour
1/4 cup soy flour
3 tablespoons lard, bacon, fat or oil
1 clove garlic, grated or 1/4 teaspoon garlic powder
1/3 cup water or broth
1-2 teaspoons nutritional yeast (optional)

Combine dry ingredients.
Add water or broth and mix well.
Roll out on a cookie sheet and bake at 350°F until golden brown.
Break in bite size chucks.

Drinks

Bourbon Slush

Audrey Schemenaur

12 ounce frozen orange juice
12 ounce frozen lemonade
4 tea bags
2 cups boiling water
2 cups bourbon
1 1/2 cups sugar
5 cups 7-UP or Sprite

Add tea bags to boiling water - let sit for few minutes
Add frozen lemonade and OJ
Add sugar, soda and bourbon
Freeze for several days

Cocoa

Mom

Makes 1 Cup

Heaping Teaspoon of Cocoa
2 heaping teaspoons of sugar
1/4 cup water
Boiling up then boil back down
Add one cup milk

Multiply this by how many cups you want.

Lime Punch

Mom

1/2 gallon lime sorbet ice cream
1 liter of 7-UP or Sprite

Mix in punch bowl and serve

Spiced Tea

Pat

1 1/4 cups instant tea
6 ounces lemonade mix (Wylers)
3 cups sugar
2 cups Tang
1 teaspoon cinnamon
1 teaspoon cloves

Add whatever it takes to a cup of hot water to achieve the taste you like.

3 Way
Pat

2 cups water
1 pounds ground beef
1 small can tomato paste
1 envelope Cincinnati Chili Mix

Put water in pan and crumble beef (raw) into water. Add tomato paste and chili mix. Simmer for several hours.

Make spaghetti and top with cheese.

All American Chili
Mom

2 pounds ground beef browned
1 large onion minced
2 gloves garlic
3-5 tablespoons chili powder
1 teaspoon salt
1 teaspoon dried oregano
1-2 teaspoon hot pepper sauce
28 ounce can crushed tomato
15 ounce can tomato sauce
30 ounce can kidney beans
1/2 cup water
1 heaping tablespoon sugar with dash of cinnamon
Simmer for several hours

BBQ Ham
Carol Lempke

5 pounds shaved ham
28 ounces Brooks ketchup
14 ounces Hunts ketchup
2 teaspoons dry mustard
1 cup brown sugar
1/2 cup sugar

Mix, simmer and serve hot on buns.

Buffalo Chicken Breasts
Eileen Tucker

14.5 ounce chicken broth
Buffalo Brand Chicken Wing Sauce
Garlic Salt
Boneless Chicken Breast

9x13 greased dish

Lay chicken breasts in dish and sprinkle with garlic salt
Pour on broth, and 1/2 bottle of buffalo sauce
Cover and bake at 325°F at least 2 hours

Chicken Casserole
Ellen Dodd

4 chicken breasts or tenders
1 box Stove Top stuffing (chicken flavored)
2 cups water
1 cup orange juice
1/2 stick butter
1/4 cup brown sugar

Mix two cups of water and stuffing in a bowl.
Put chicken in a 9 x 13 dish.
Put dressing mixture over chicken.
Mix the OJ, butter and sugar and pour over chicken and dressing.

Bake at 350°F for 45 - 60 minutes until chicken is done

Chicken Rolls

Becki

2 chicken breasts (cooked and cut into small pieces)
8 ounce cream cheese
Dash sage
Crescent rolls
Butter
Stuffing mix

Mix chicken, cream cheese, and sage
Separate rolls and put in chicken mixture and seal
Dip in butter and roll in stuffing mix

Bake 30 minutes at 350°F

Chris' Turkey Chili

Chris ("the Janitor") Goepper

Package ground turkey
1 large onion
28 ounce can crushed tomatoes
28 ounce can diced tomatoes (or petite diced)
14 ounce can black beans
14 ounce can kidney beans
14 ounce can white beans (or navy)
Chili powder
Salt
Garlic powder

Brown meat in some water.
Pour off water and chop up as desired.
Dice up the onion into your size pieces.
Dump in the tomatoes and drained beans.
Season to taste with chili powder, salt and garlic powder.
Cook on low heat until done.

Serve with cheese and crackers and a nice table wine.

Now for the variation:
Of course all ingredients subject to change based upon the cook's current state of mind.
So we'll call the next section the "Agents of Change".
"Agents of Change"
Chopped celery
Chopped pepper (green, yellow and/or red)
Chopped jalapeno's
Chopped mushrooms
Ground beef instead of turkey
Lots more onion.

At Liberty tax, Chris defers the table wine until after hours, but when he's away - the cats do play.

Egg/Sausage Casserole

Katie Noppert

2-3 cups of croutons
1 1/2 pounds browned sausage
2 1/2 cups shredded cheese (mild cheddar)
3/4 teaspoon dry mustard
5 eggs
2 1/2 cups milk
1 can cream of mushroom (or celery or chicken) soup and 1/2 can of milk

9 x 13 greased dish
Line bottom of dish with croutons
Sprinkle cheese on top
Beat eggs, 2 1/2 cups milk and dry mustard
Pour over cheese
Add sausage
Cover and refrigerate over night

Before baking dilute soup with 1/2 can of milk
Pour over sausage

Bake at 300°F for one hour

Enchilada Casserole
Pat

1 pound ground beef or sausage
1 teaspoon oregano
1/2 teaspoon salt
1 clove garlic
16 ounce can of tomato sauce
10 ounce can enchilada sauce
12 tortilla
1 onion chopped
1 pound grated cheese
Black olives

Brown meat, oregano, salt, garlic
Stir in tomatoes and enchilada sauce
in pan
Dip tortilla in sauce
Combine onion cheese and olives
Layer dipped tortilla, meat & cheese

Bake 350°F 30-40 minutes

Fried Chicken
Aunt Flo

1/3 cup flour
1 Teaspoon paprika
1 Teaspoon Salt
1/4 Teaspoon Pepper
2 eggs
1/2 cup milk
Chicken
Shortening for frying
Mix eggs and milk

Combine flour, paprika, salt, and pepper in plastic bag
Dredge chicken thru milk then put in flour mixture.
Add two or three pieces of chicken at a time and shake
Heat shortening 1/4 inch deep in skillet
After all pieces are browned cover and cook until tender (30 to 40 minutes). Uncover last 10 minutes.
Add a little water if needed

Grilled Cheese in a Pan
Becki

8 ounce tube crescent rolls
1 cup each of:
Colby, Cheddar, Mozzarella, & Monterey Cheeses
1 8 ounce package cream cheese
1 egg
1 tablespoon butter
1 tablespoon sesame seeds

8 x 8 baking dish
Put 1/2 of crescent rolls in bottom of dish

Combine the shredded cheeses and put in dish
Cut up cream cheese and place on top of shredded cheeses

Put other 1/2 of crescent rolls on top of cream cheese

Spread melted butter on top and sprinkle sesame seeds.
Bake at 350°F for 15-20 minutes or until rolls are browned.

Lamb Roast
Pat

3-4 pound of Leg of Lamb
Heat Oven 325°F
Season Lamb with salt and pepper
Place fat side up on rack in open
roasting pan: do not add water
Cook for 3 to 3.5 hours (meat
thermometer should be at 175°-180°)
Let roast stand for 15 minutes before
carving

Lasagna - Meatless
Pat

6 ounces of lasagna noodles
1/4 teaspoon dried oregano
15 1/2 ounce can spaghetti sauce
(with or without meat)
1 cup small curd cottage cheese
6 ounce package sliced mozzarella
cheese

Cook noodles

Add oregano to spaghetti sauce,
then add cottage cheese
In greased 8 x 8 dish add half
noodles, half spaghetti sauce and
half mozzarella cheese
Repeat next layer
Bake at 375°F for about 30 minutes
Let stand 10 minutes before serving

Mostaccioli & Meatballs
Pat

Meatballs
1 pound ground beef
1/2 pound ground pork
2/3 - 3/4 cup oats

1 egg
8 ounces of tomato sauce
2 cups of Mozzarella Cheese
Small onion
Mix all these ingredients together
and brown in a skillet.

Sauce
Put 3-4 Tablespoons oil in the
bottom of a large pot
add 1-2 gloves of crushed garlic
Brown slightly
Add :
3 15 ounce cans of tomato sauce
2 12 ounce cans of tomato paste
2 cans of water
Stir until blended
Add:
1/2 container of Parm Plus (or
parmesan cheese)
8 ounces of pepperoni

Put meatballs in sauce and let
simmer for several hours.

When ready to eat make Mostaccioli
noodles and sprinkle with fresh
grated parmesan cheese. Enjoy.
This makes enough to feed 10-12
adults who are hungry.

Peachy Bean Skillet
Ellen Dodd

1 pound kielbasa cut into coin
slices - then quartered
2 15 ounces cans pork and beans
29 ounces can sliced cling peaches,
drained
1/2 cup firmly packed brown sugar
1/2 cup ketchup
Brown kielbasa in skillet

Add:
pork and beans, ketchup, and brown sugar
Heat on medium-low for 10 minutes
Add peaches - heat until peaches are warm (5-10 minutes)

Peanut Butter & Jelly Sandwich
Pat

1 Tablespoon Peanut Butter
1 Tablespoon Jam
2 Slices White Bread
1 Complaining Child

Apply peanut butter to first slice of bread.
Apply jam to second slice of bread.
Bring each slice together, with the filling on the inside, to form a sandwich.
Give to complaining child.

Poppy Seed Chicken
Pat

4 large chicken or turkey breasts
1 bay leaf
2 cans cream of mushroom soup
16 ounce sour cream
1 Tablespoon Worcestershire sauce
Pepper to taste
2 packages of Ritz crackers, crushed in plastic bag until fine
1 stick of butter melted
1/4 cup poppy seeds

Preheat oven to 350°F
Cover chicken with water, add bay leaf and simmer until done.
After chicken cools, cut into bite size pieces

Mix soup, sour cream, Worcestershire sauce and pepper.
Place chicken in an 11 x 13 baking dish and pour soup mixture over chicken.
Top with crushed crackers and pour melted butter over top. Sprinkle with poppy seeds
Bake 25 to 30 minutes or until top is golden brown.

Pork Roast
Pat

Pork Loin Center Loin 3-4 pounds
Salt and pepper
Fat side up - meat browns as it cooks
Bake at 325°F for 2 1/2 - 3 hours
Meat thermometer should be at 170°

Prime Rib
Pat

1 semi-boneless beef rib roast (4-6 pounds)
1 Tablespoon olive oil
1 - 2 Teaspoons coarsely ground pepper

Horseradish Sauce
1 cup sour cream
3 - 4 Tablespoons horseradish
1 Teaspoon coarsely ground pepper
splash of Worcestershire sauce

Brush roast with oil; rub with pepper. Place roast fat side up in shallow baking dish. Bake uncovered for 15 minutes at 450°F.
Reduce heat to 325°F. Bake for 2 3/4 hours or until meat reaches doneness (for rare a meat

thermometer should read 140°, medium rare 145°, medium 160°, well done 170°). Baste with pan dripping every 30 minutes.
Let stand for 10-15 minutes before slicing. Roast will continue cooking when removed from oven.
In a small bowl combine the sauce ingredients. Serve with beef.

Ribs
Pat

Heat oven to 325°F
Cover ribs with Montgomery Inn BBQ sauce.
Cook for 2 hours - covered with foil

Grill for several minutes on both sides

Roast Beef and Gravy
Pat

3-4 pound chuck roast
Melt 2 Tablespoons of butter in the bottom of a pressure cooker.
Brown roast on both sides

Add:
5 cups of water
6 beef bouillon cubes
1 onion
Salt and pepper

Cook in pressure cooker for 45 minutes (follow the directions for cool down)

Gravy:
2 cup COLD water (I put the water in the fridge while the meat is cooking.
4 Tablespoons flour

Mix well, add slowly to the juice left in the pan after removing meat.
Cook until thick.
This can be served as hot roast beef sandwiches or with mashed potatoes and gravy.

Southern Fried Chicken
Aunt Flo

Combine:
1/2 cup flour
1/4 teaspoon pepper
1 teaspoon paprika
1 1/2 teaspoons salt

Dredge chicken in flour mixture
Brown in shortening then reduce heat and cook for 30 minutes (I use an electric skillet for this).

Spaghetti Casserole
Bev Droege

1 large jar spaghetti sauce
7 ounces of spaghetti
2 eggs
1/2 cup milk
4 ounce package of cheddar cheese
1 pound ground beef or Italian sausage (browned)
1 teaspoon oregano
2 packages 8 ounce sliced mozzarella cheese

Cook spaghetti and put in 9 x 13 dish
Beat eggs and milk and pour on spaghetti
Add meat and oregano
Add spaghetti sauce
Top with mozzarella cheese

Bake at 350°F for 45 minutes

Taco Bake
Ellen Dodd

2 pounds ground beef
1/2 cup chopped onion
15 ounce can tomato sauce
15 ounce can kidney beans, drained
2 teaspoons chili powder
1 1/2 teaspoons salt
1/2 teaspoon pepper
1 package taco shell (12 shells)
2 cups shredded cheddar or
Monterey
Taco sauce
Shredded lettuce
Grape tomatoes

Brown beef and onion, stir in tomato
sauce, kidney beans, chili powder,
salt and pepper.
Break up taco shells into bottom of 9
x 13 dish.
Spoon meat mixture over shells.
Top with cheese
Bake at 350°F for 15-20 minutes

Taco Pasta
Becki

16 ounces fettuccine pasta cooked
1 pound ground beef or chicken
browned and drained
1 package taco seasoning
4 ounces cheddar cheese
1 can sliced tomatoes

Salt, pepper, garlic powder and
parmesan cheese to taste
Mix everything together and serve
immediately with sour cream

Tilapia
Pat

4 tilapia fillets (about 1 pound)
2 tablespoons oil
2 tablespoons lime juice
zest of two limes
1 tablespoon fresh basil, minced
2 teaspoons bourbon
1 teaspoon salt
pepper to taste.

Combine all ingredients except
tilapia fillets in resealable plastic bag.
Turn to mix and add tilapia.
Seal and refrigerate for at least 30
minutes.
GRILL each tilapia fillet for about 3
minutes per side.. The marinade can
be boiled and served on fish if
desired.

Vodka Pasta
Mike Padenich

1 cup vodka
3/4 stick butter
1 teaspoon crushed red pepper
flakes
Simmer in pan for 5 minutes

14.5 ounce can diced tomatoes
1 cup heavy cream
Salt and pepper to taste
Add to above and cook for 5 minutes

Add one pound of cooked bowtie
wheat pasta

Mix in 6 - 8 ounces of Romano or
parmesan cheese

Yum-A-Setta

Pat

2 pounds of ground beef
Salt and pepper to taste
1/4 cup brown sugar
1/4 cup onion
Brown these ingredients
1 can tomato soup
1 can cream of chicken soup
16 ounces of cooked egg noodles
Mix these 3 ingredients together
8 ounces Velveeta cheese

9 x13 baking dish
Layer beef mixture, noodle mixture
and cheese. Should make two layers

Bake 350°F for 1/2 hours

Other

Ground Hog's Day
Rick "Basset Dad" Miller

1 woodchuck
2 onions, sliced
1/2 cup celery
Flour
Vinegar and water
Salt and pepper
Cloves
Clean woodchuck - remove glands;
cut into serving pieces.
Soak overnight in a solution of equal
parts of water and vinegar with one
slice onion and a little salt.
Drain, wash, and wipe.
Parboil for 20 minutes, drain and
cover with fresh boiling water.
Add onion, celery, a few cloves and
salt and pepper to taste.
Cook until tender; thicken gravy with
flour.

Pie Crust
Little Grammy

2/3 cup Crisco
2 cups flour
5-6 tablespoons cold water
1 teaspoon salt

Put all these ingredients in a bowl
and knead until mixed (I use my
hands)

Form into two equal balls
Roll out using as much flour at you
need so that it doesn't stick to the
rolling pin or flat surface.

Fold in half and then slide into pie
plate

After filling pie, repeat this process
and slide on top.
Pinch the two crusts together.

Put several vent holes in crust
Use 1 tablespoon milk to coat the top
of pie and then sprinkle with
granulated sugar before baking

Thelma's Bread and Butter Pickles
"Little" Grammy

1 gallon cucumbers
8 small white onions
2 green peppers
Above all sliced thin
1/2 cup salt
1 quart crushed ice
Let stand 3 hours and then drain

5 cups sugar
2 tablespoons mustard seed
1 1/2 teaspoons turmeric
1 teaspoon celery seed
1/2 teaspoon ground cloves
5 cups vinegar

Mix these ingredients with cucumber
mixture, bring all to a boil over slow
fire, put in quart jars and seal.

Salad

Ambrosia or 6 Cup Salad

Ellen Dodd

1 cup pineapple chunks
1 cup red or green grapes - halved
1 cup mandarin orange
1 cup sour cream
1 cup shredded coconut
1 cup mini marshmallows

Mix well and chill

Banana Salad

Granny Tucker

1/2 cup sugar
2 well beaten eggs
1 teaspoon apple cider vinegar
3 teaspoons flour
2 tablespoons butter

Cook above ingredients over low heat until thick (about 2-3 minutes)

Add 5-6 pounds sliced bananas

Place in bowl

Top with crushed peanuts

Refrigerate until cool

BLT Salad

Sheila Byrd

1 Head lettuce
2 chopped tomatoes
8 slices cooked bacon - crumbled
1 bunch of green onion chopped
Mayo

Rinse and dry lettuce, tear into pieces

Add tomatoes, bacon and onions

Enough mayo to coat salad.

Serve immediately.

Broccoli Salad

Kathy Jones Kinslow

2 heads of broccoli cut into small pieces
diced onion to taste
1/2 pound bacon cooked and broken up
1/2 - 1 cup pecans
1/2 cup raisins

Sauce
1 cup mayo
2 teaspoon vinegar
1/2 cup sugar

Mix and stir into above ingredients and refrigerate overnight

Stir before serving

Caesar Salad

Pat

1 coddled egg (or 1heaping teaspoon of mayo)
Salt
2 cloves garlic
1 ounce can of anchovies
1 ounce Worcestershire sauce
1 cup olive oil
2 tablespoons lemon juice
6 teaspoons parmesan cheese
3 whole peppercorns
Romaine lettuce

Salad

Croutons

Sprinkle salt on bottom of salad bowl
Mash anchovies and mix with
Worcestershire sauce, oil, lemon, 3
tablespoons cheese, pepper, add
coddled egg and remainig cheese.

Pour over lettuce and toss - add
croutons

Cauliflower & Bacon Salad
Pat

1 head lettuce
1 head cauliflower
1 small red onion
1/2 pound bacon
1 cup mayo
1/3 cup parmesan cheese
3 tablespoons sugar

Layer lettuce, cauliflower, onion,
bacon
Combine remaining ingredients and
spread over salad
Refrigerate
Toss before serving

Chicken Salad
Pat

3-4 chicken breasts
6 hardboiled eggs
1/2 small onion or one bunch of
green onions minced
25 red grapes halved
2 cups mayo
1 tablespoon pickle relish
1 tablespoon mustard
Salt and pepper to taste

Cook chicken breasts until tender (I
use a pressure cooker - they are
done in 10 minutes - 15 if frozen).
Shred up chicken in bowl
Cut up eggs
Add minced onions, halved grapes,
pickle relish, mustard, salt and
pepper.
Coat all with mayo.
Can be served on crackers, bread or
with veggies.

Orange Cream Fruit Salad
Mom

20 ounces pineapple chunks
16 ounces sliced peaches
11 ounces mandarin oranges
2 large bananas
1 small box vanilla instant pudding
1 1/2 cups milk
1/3 cup frozen orange juice
3/4 cup sour cream

Mix all drained fruit (except bananas)
Beat pudding, milk and orange juice
for 2 minutes and then add sour
cream and mix well
Spoon over fruit and toss to coat
Cover and refrigerate for 2 hours
Add bananas just before serving

Oriental Coleslaw
Pam Elliott

16 ounce package coleslaw mix
1 bunch green onions
1/4 cup package sunflower seeds
2 packages sliced almonds toasted
2 packages oriental ramen noodles,
crushed, save seasoning for dressing
Combine the above in a large bowl

Dressing
1/3 cup sugar
3/4 cup vegetable oil
1/4 cup white vinegar
Seasoning saved from ramen
noodles

Combine all ingredients in bowl. Stir
dressing well before pouring over
slaw - put on slaw just before serving.

Seven Layer Salad

Bev Eiding

Lettuce (of choice) chopped
3/4 cup frozen peas
1 cup cut up broccoli
1/2 pound fried and crumbled bacon
2 hard boiled eggs
1/2 can kidney beans drained
onions to taste
sunflower seeds/pumpkins seeds
(whatever you like)
Mozzarella Cheese
Little ranch dressing
Small clumps of Hellmann's Mayo
Parmesan cheese

In 9 x13 dish start with lettuce and
then add each layer. You can add
whatever veggies or seeds you like.

Strawberry Salad

Julie Schilling

10 cups spinach or romaine lettuce
2 cups strawberries
1 cup pecans or similar nuts
1/2 cup purple onion

Dressing

1/2 cup olive oil
2-3 tablespoons apple cider vinegar
2-3 tablespoons sugar
1 tablespoon lemon juice
1 tablespoon poppy seeds
1/2 teaspoon salt
1/2 teaspoon ground mustard

Mix dressing well and allow to sit a
while before using.
When ready toss with greens

Strawberry Spinach Salad

Pam Elliott

10 ounce bag fresh spinach
1 quart strawberries
1 package sliced almonds, toasted

Mix together
1/2 cups oil
1/2 cup sugar
1/4 cup red wine vinegar
1 tablespoon sesame seeds
1 teaspoon poppy seeds
1 teaspoon Worcestershire

Toss over, spinach , strawberries,
and almonds

Strawberry/Pretzel

Granny Tucker

Crush 2 cups pretzels
1 stick butter
3 tablespoons brown sugar

Mix these ingredients and press into
a 9 x 13
Bake 15 minutes 350°F and chill

16 ounce cool whip

8 ounce softened cream cheese
1 cup confectionary sugar

Mix these ingredients and spread
over crust - return to fridge

1 large red Jell-O (flavor your choice)
1 cup boiling water
1 box frozen strawberries

Mix and layer on top of cream
cheese mixture

Let gel for several hours

Baked Macaroni and Cheese

Pat

Cook 3 cups of macaroni according to package directions
1 stick butter
Velveeta cheese
Sour cream
Cushed crackers

Melt butter and cheese in pan.

Remove from heat and stir in sour cream.

Stir in cooked macaroni and place in baking dish.
Put crackers on top.
Cook for 30-40 minutes at 350°F

Broccoli & Cauliflower Casserole

Pat

Cut up:
1 head of Broccoli
1 head of Cauliflower
2 bunches of green onions
1/2 pound cooked bacon

Put in large bowl

Dressing:
1 cup mayo (Hellmann's)
1/3 cup red wine vinegar
1/2 cup sugar
1 teaspoon seasoning salt
1/4 teaspoon pepper
Mix these ingredients together and toss over veggies.

Carrots au Gratin

Vickie Pollock Jellison

3 cups cooked carrots
1/2 cup water
1/2 cup Velveeta cheese
2 tablespoons butter
Pepper to taste
1/4 cup green pepper
1 teaspoon onion salt
15 soda crackers

After cooking carrots, combine all the other ingredients and top with soda crackers.

Cook for 15-20 minutes at 425°F

Corn Casserole

Pat

2 eggs
15 ounce can whole corn, drained
15 ounce can cream corn
1 stick butter, melted
8 ounces sour cream
1 Box Jiffy corn bread mix

Preheat oven 350°F
Spray 9 x 13 baking dish with "Pam"

Beat eggs
Add whole corn, cream corn, butter, sour cream, and corn bread mix.
Blend well.

Pour into greased dish and bake 1 hour or until knife comes out clean.

Country Corn Bake
Ellen Dodd

5 slices bacon
20 ounce bag corn, thawed and drained
1 can cream of potato soup
1/2 cup milk
1/2 cup celery
1 tablespoon pimiento
1/2 teaspoon seasoned salt
1/2 cup cheddar cheese
1 can French's French Fried onions

Combine corn, soup, milk, celery, pimiento, salt, 1/2 cup cheese, 1/2 can fried onions, 3 slices bacon and put in 8" square baking dish.

Bake at 375°F covered for 40-45 minutes.

Top with remaining bacon, cheese and onions.

Bake uncovered another 3 minutes or until onions are brown.

Cranberry Jell-O Salad
Julie Schilling

3 small packages of strawberry Jell-O
20 1/4 cups hot water
3/4 can crushed pineapple in its own juice
1 can whole cranberry sauce
10 ounce package frozen strawberry
Allow frozen strawberries to thaw in fridge.
Mix Jell-O with water, while still warm mix cranberry sauce in.
Add pineapple with the juice and then the strawberries.

Mix well and refrigerate until solid (usually overnight)

Deviled eggs
Big Grammy

Hard boil six eggs
Cut in half and place whites on dish.
Put yellows in a separate bowl.

Mush up yellows of eggs with a fork.
Add salt and pepper to taste
Mix 1/2 cup mayo & 1 tablespoon mustard.

With teaspoon scoop yellow egg mixtures into white.

Homemade Noodles
Grandma Schilling

4 eggs
2 cups flour
Mix these thoroughly.
The dough will be sticky.
Divide into two ball using lots of flour to keep your hands from sticky to dough.
Roll out the dough as thin as possible.
Cover with flour and turn several times during this process.
When rolled out thin, cut into four pieces.
Stack the four pieces on top of each other (again use flour so the pieces don't stick together).
Roll up and then slice into 1/2 pieces.
Repeat with second ball.

Bring water to boil in a large pot. Add

noodles and bring back to a boil.
Let boil for 1 minute stirring
constantly.
Rinse with cold water.

Broth:
4 beef or chicken bouillon cubes
4 cups water.

After bouillon dissolves, add cooked
noodles and let simmer for one half
hour.

Hot Fruit Compote

Pat

2 apples peeled and cubed
20 ounce can pineapple chunks
15 ounce can sliced pears
15 ounce can sliced peaches
1 can whole-berry cranberry sauce
1/4 cup packed brown sugar
1 teaspoon ground cinnamon
1/4 teaspoon ground ginger
1/4 teaspoon ground cloves

In 2 quart baking dish coated with
Pam, combine fruit.
In small bowl, combine cranberry
sauce, brown sugar, cinnamon,
ginger and cloves.
Stir into fruit
Cover and bake at 350°F for 45-55
minutes or until bubbly.

Mashed Potatoes

Pat

Cook 2 1/2 pounds of red potatoes
(peeled and quartered) until tender
Put in bowl that you can use electric
beaters in.

Beat the cooked potatoes with 1 stick
of butter, two cloves of garlic and 1
1/2 - 2 cups of sour cream
Salt and pepper to taste.

Pineapple Dish

Mom

1 large can of crushed pineapple
drained (save juice)
1 cup grated cheddar cheese
3/4 cup sugar
2 tablespoons flour
1 cup bread crumbs
1/3 cup butter

Mix pineapple and cheese and put in
greased 8x8 baking dish
Mix sugar, flour and pineapple juice
and pour over mixture
Top with bread crumbs and pour
melted butter over top
Bake for 45 minutes at 350°F

This dish is awesome with ham

Potato Pancakes

Pat

1/4 cup milk or sour cream
2 eggs
3 cups finely chopped potatoes
1 finely chopped small onion
3 tablespoons flour
1 teaspoon salt
1/4 teaspoon baking powder

Put all ingredients in blender for 15
seconds.

Pour in hot skillet like you would
pancakes, flip when brown.

Potato Salad
Big Grammy

7 red potatoes
5 hard boiled eggs
1 bunch of green onion (or white onion)
1 1/2 cup mayo
2 tablespoon mustard
Salt and Pepper to taste
Optional:
Celery
Bacon

Cook potatoes until tender - peel and cut into bit size pieces.
Cut up hard boiled eggs
Add the rest of the ingredients and make sure all potatoes are coated with the mayo and mustard mix.

Spike's Spaghetti Melt
Becki Schilling Droege

1 pound spaghetti
2 pound box Velveeta cheese
Milk

Cook spaghetti according to directions

Layer 1/2 of spaghetti in 9 x 13 pan with 1/2 of cheese cut into big chunks
Other half of spaghetti and cheese
Pour enough milk in - just over 1/2 full
Cook at 350°F for 1 hour covered.
Uncover and cook until cheese is browned.

Sweet Potato Pie
Julie Schilling

4 cups mashed sweet potatoes (4 medium potatoes)
1 teaspoon vanilla
2 well beaten eggs
1/2 stick butter
3/4 cup honey
1 tablespoon coconut oil to grease pan

Boil potatoes with skins for 25-30 minutes or until tender. Remove. Let cool and peel.
Mix all ingredients and pour into greased 9 x 13 dish.

1 cup chopped pecans or almonds
1/2 cup flour
3/4 cup honey
3/4 stick butter
Combine all ingredients and sprinkle over top.

Bake at 350°F for 30 minutes

Munchies

Pat Ziegler

1 package (18 ounces) granola
without raisins
1 can (17 ounces) mixed nuts
1 package (15 ounces) raisins
1 package (14 ounces) milk
chocolate M&M's
1 package (14 ounces) peanut
M&M's
1 package (12 1/4 ounces) Honey
Nut Cheerios
1 package (8.9 ounces) Cheerios

Mix together in large bowl and store
in cover container or large resealable
plastic bags.

Broccoli/Cauliflower Soup
Pat

Cook head of EITHER Broccoli or Cauliflower (either one tastes great). Mush up before adding to soup

2 Cans cream of chicken soup
1/2 cup French onion dip or sour cream
2 teaspoons onion diced
2 tablespoons butter (melted)
1 tablespoon flour
Parmesan cheese - to taste
Velveeta cheese - to taste
1 can water

Mix all the ingredients with the cooked veggie of choice and place in large cookware and heat in oven at 350°F for 45 minutes stirring occasionally.

I threw this recipe together one day with "stuff" I had around the house. Makes a huge amount.

Potato Soup or Vichyssoise
Pat

4 cups chicken broth
4 cups chopped potatoes
1/4 cup diced onions
1 1/2 teaspoons salt
8 ounce cream cheese
1 tablespoon chopped chives

In large sauce pan, combine broth, potatoes, onion and salt.
Bring to a boil.
Cover and simmer for 20 minutes.
Mush mixture up.

Gradually add cream cheese mixing until well blended. Stir in chives.
Can be served hot or cold.

Ammonia
Pat Ziegler

Put 1/2 cup ammonia with hot water in pans that are extremely "food burnt". Wait about 1/2 hour and the clean up will be faster

Baking Soda
Pat

General Purpose Cleaner
1 teaspoon Borax
1 teaspoon baking soda
2 teaspoons vinegar or lemon juice
1/4 teaspoon liquid dish soap
2 cups hot water
Mix and store in a squirt or spray bottle

Grease Cutter Cleanup
Great for grease buildup on stove, backsplashes or enamel surfaces
1/4 cup baking soda
1/2 cup white vinegar
1 cup ammonia
1 gallon hot water
Wear rubber gloves and use in a well ventilated area

Sprinkle baking soda on a damp sponge, and scrub your fruit and veggies to remove dirt, wax or pesticide residue. Rinse well.

Silver Tarnish Remover
Boil water and 1/2 teaspoon salt with 1 to 2 teaspoons of baking soda. Place tarnished silverware in pan with boiled mixture and a piece of aluminum foil. Simmer for 2 - 3 minutes. Rinse the silverware well,

then use a soft cloth to dry.

Basic Bathroom Cleaner
3 tablespoons baking soda
4 tablespoons dishwashing liquid
2 cups warm water
Mix well and store in sealed container

Showerhead treatment
1/2 cup baking soda
1 cup vinegar
Mix in a sturdy plastic bag, then secure the bag around the showerhead with a rubber band so that the showerhead is submerged in the solution. Keep on and soak for one hour. Remove and run very hot water thru the shower head for several minutes.

Odor Control
Musty smelling laundry should be washed and then add 1/2 cup baking soda to the rinse cycle.

Air Freshener: Put baking soda in a pretty dish or basket and add your favorite scented bath salts to the mix. Change every three months.

Add 1/2 cup baking soda with your detergent to freshen your laundry and help liquid detergents work harder

Add 1/2 cup baking soda (only 1/4 cup for front loading machines) with the usual amount of bleach to increase whitening power.

Remove cigarette smoke smells in the clothes by soaking them in a baking soda solution before washing.

Tips

Crayons in the wash - rewash the load in the hottest water possible, adding 1/2 - 1 box of baking soda. Repeat if necessary.

Give your dog a dry bath by sprinkling him/her with baking soda. Rub in, then brush out.
For a wet wash, combine 3 tablespoons baking soda with 1 teaspoon dishwashing liquid and 1 teaspoon baby oil in a spray bottle. Spritz your pet, then wipe dry.

Brownies
Pat

When making boxed brownies, add chocolate syrup and/or chocolate chips.

Buttor
Pat Ziegler

Anywhere in this recipe that it called for butter - I use real butter - never oleo

Cake from Box
Pat

Use milk instead of water - yum - richer.

Cat Hair
Pat

Put on a pair of rubber gloves and go to town on fabric by just rubbing your gloved hand over the fabric. A quick way to remove hair.

Cookie Bars
Pat Ziegler

Almost every butter-sugar-flour cookie you can think of can be adapted for cookie bars. Peanut Butter, oatmeal, chocolate chips etc. For most bars, your recipe is as easy as this: Press your favorite cookie dough into a foil lined pan (if you make the foil extra long you can scrunch up and make handles for easier lifting out of pan) and bake for 20-30 minutes.

Things to know about cookie bars. It's all about butter. Good cookie bars depend on good butter. That chewy center, those crispy corners - they are both thanks to butter. So don't skimp. Buy good quality butter - no substitutions.
Freeze freely. Once they cool, wrap your bars tightly in plastic wrap, then aluminum foil. Most will freeze for up to two months. You can even freeze then individually so you can take out one at a time.

Dog Bath for Skunk Smell
Pat

1 quart of 3 percent hydrogen peroxide
1/4 cup of baking soda
1 teaspoon liquid castile soap (available at health food stores). I used Dawn dishing liquid the one time I did this.
Mix all ingredients in a medium size bucket because it will fizz.
Soak your dog's fur, being careful

not to get the solution in her eyes, nose, ears or mouth.
These ingredients are natural, but they have acidic properties and can cause irritation.
Knead the solution into the fur, covering every part of the dog. It is important to soak well, especially for long haired dogs.
Use a sponge around the eyes and head. Rinse thoroughly, and dry the dog.
This solution changes the chemical properties of the skunk spray to break it down, so the odor is eliminated, not masked.
Throw any left over solution away.

Green Clean - Furniture Polish
Pat

1 cup mineral oil
1 cup white vinegar

Stir or shake to mix, wipe on with a clean cloth

Mayo
Pat Ziegler

Anywhere in this cookbook that a recipe calls for mayo, I use Hellmann's.

Rice Krispies Treats
Pat

Use 4 tablespoons of butter instead of 3. Makes the treats more moist and chewy.

Tips
Pat

To keep potatoes from budding, place an apple in the bag with the potatoes

To prevent egg shells from cracking, add a pinch of salt to water before hard boiling

Run your hands under cold water before pressing Rice Krispies treats into the pan to keep the marshmallow from sticking to fingers

If you accidentally add to much salt while cooking, drop a peeled potato in the mix - it absorbs the excess salt for an instant "fix me up"

Place an apple in hardened brown sugar to soften it back up

When boiling corn on the cob, add a pinch of sugar to help bring out the corns natural sweetness

Headache? - Take a lime, cut in half and rub it on your forehead, throbbing goes away

Adding mayo to cake recipes (1/2 water 1/2 mayo) makes for a moister cake instead of all water.

Vinegar - White
Pat

Countertops
Wipe your countertops with undiluted vinegar once a day to shine them and keep your kitchen smelling fresh.

Tips

Clogs
A mixture of equal parts vinegar, salt and baking soda may help open a slow-draining sink. Pour solution down drain; let it sit for 1 hour, then pour boiling water down drain.

Toilets
Pour vinegar into toilet and let sit for 30 minutes. Next sprinkle baking soda on a toilet bowl brush and scour any remaining stained area. Flush.

Floors
Ceramic Tile
Mop with a mixture of 1 cup vinegar to 1 gallon warm water to make ceramic tile floor sparkle
Linoleum and vinyl
Scrub a linoleum floor with a mixture of 1 gallon water with 1 cup vinegar. If floor needs a polish after this, use club soda.
Wood
Add a cup of vinegar to a gallon bucket of water, and mop lightly onto hardwood floors (do not saturate). No need to rinse. This will keep floors shiny and remove any greasy buildup.

Laundry
Vinegar is a powerhouse when it comes to pretreating stains, softening water, and boosting regular laundry detergents.
Clothes softener:
Add 1/2 cup vinegar to the last rinse cycle of your wash to soften clothes.
Lint:
Reduce lint buildup and keep pet hair from clinging to clothing by adding vinegar to last rinse cycle.
Static Cling
A good way to control static cling is to add 1/2 cup vinegar to last rinse cycle
Keeping Colors Colorful:
Any colored clothing item that has become dulled can be brightened by soaking it in 1 gallon warm water and 1 cup vinegar. Follow this with a clear water rinse.

Litter Boxes
Use vinegar to clean out a kitty litter pan. Remove litter, and pour in 1/2 inch of vinegar. Let sit for 15 minutes. Pour out, and thoroughly dry pan. Then sprinkle with baking soda and add fresh litter.

Recipe Substitutes
Buttermilk:
Stir 1 tablespoon vinegar into 1 cup of whole milk and let stand a few minutes.

Lemons and Limes
Vinegar can be used in any recipe calling for lemon or lime juice. Use 1/2 teaspoon vinegar for each teaspoon of lemon or lime.

Salt:
Instead of salt, use vinegar as a seasoning for food such as potatoes or veggies. Just sprinkle on lightly.

Safe way to clean diamonds
Soak diamonds in a small bowl filled with equal parts of vinegar and warm water. While the jewelry is soaking, brush with a soft toothbrush. Rinse under warm running water. Pat dry with a soft lint free cloth.

WD 40

Carol Flanigan

WD40 who knew. "Water Displacement #40". The product began from a search for a rust preventative solvent and degreaser to protect missile parts. WD-40 was created in 1953 by three technicians at the San Diego Rocket Chemical Company. They were successful with the fortieth formulation, thus WD-40. Following are some interesting uses for WD-40 and before you say "YUCK" know that the main ingredient in WD40 is FISH OIL.

1. Protects silver from tarnishing (of course, you need to start with it all ready polished).
2. Removes road tar and grime from cars
3. Gives floors the "just waxed" sheen without making them slippery.
4. Keeps flies off cows
5. Restores and cleans chalkboards
6. Removes lipstick stains.
7. Untangles jewelry chains
8. Removes stains from stainless steel sinks
9. Removes tomato stains from clothing
10. Keeps shower doors free of water spots.
11. Restores and cleans padded leather dashboards in vehicles, as well as vinyl bumpers
12. Removes splatter grease on stove
13. Keeps bathroom mirrors from fogging
14. Removes traces of duct tape
15. Folks even spray it on their arms, hands, and knees to relieve arthritis
16. Removes crayon from walls

This is in addition to all the normal uses for removing rust to "greasing" the tracts.

Biographies

Audrey Schemenaur

Birthday   8/6/1928

Audrey was my mother's maid of honor in their wedding. She is a hoot to be around and her slush is the best - you should definilty try it. Her husband, Andy, worked at the shop for years after he retired. He was the truck driver - We miss him!! Audy is a great friend to my mom and dad, as well as me. She is just so much fun to be around but she never learned to drive so you have to go to her.

Aunt Flo

Birthday   11/22/1899

Aunt Flo was "Big Grammy's" oldest sister. She lived on the "farm" in the house she was born in all her life. And lived to be 95 years old. One of the special highlights of my youth was spending time each summer with her. Aunt Flo on the farm every summer. Aunt Flo and Uncle Clarence (married to her sister, my Aunt Freda) owned a creamery together. Once a week during the summer, Aunt Flo and I would go to all the little country stores and deliver the best cheese I have ever eaten and butter for the stores to sell to their customers.
Aunt Flo was an incredible influence in many people's lives and I am so grateful that I - and my children were some of them.

Aunt Freda

Birthday   11/2/1905

Aunt Freda was the fourth of the Ellinghausen children to which my father descended from. She was married to Uncle Clarence until his death in 1972. While spending time with Aunt Flo every summer, I also would go to Aunt Freda for a while. She had a tabacco basin and I helped her pick off the worms on the plants. They made for great fishing and Uncle Clarence would clean the fish and Aunt Freda would fry them for dinner. I also got to collect the eggs each morning and slop the hogs. I truly loved the farm life.

Aunt Freda had a great sense of humor. Really can't share any with you because it wouldn't be politically correct, she was a hoot though. She also had a shot of whiskey everyday to keep her healthy.

Becki Schilling Droege

Birthday   9/30/1970

I've know Becki since she was born. In case you don't know me, she is my only daughter. She has graced me with 3 charming grandchildren (Wyatt, Ainsley, & Mycah), which I love dearly. I'd like to tell you that everything Becki has learned came from me, but not so. She is a very talented person, just check out her scrapbooking. She also has patience, which I am really lacking in (I take after Papa Dale). She sees the good in everyone and wants to "fix" everything. I am so proud of her.

Biographies

Bev Eiding

Birthday   3/16/1949

Bev and I grew up together in Sayler Park. As children we would spend the summers playing canasta and swimming. As adults we lived across the street from one another for years. All our children were/are friends. Bev and I were Girl Scout Co-Leaders for Becki and Kari.

Bev and I still play canasta with a mother and daughter duo (Ellen and Erika). It's always a pleasure to be with Bev as she is one of the most positive people I have ever known and is a real inspiration to me and many others.

Big Grammy

Birthday   9/17/1903

Helen Ziegler (aka Big Grammy) was my paternal grandmother. She was raised on the farm in Indiana with her 3 sisters (Flo, Freda, & Etta) and one brother (Alec). She married Cliff Ziegler and had three sons (Dale, Bill & Chuck). She is the only sibling to have children.

Carol Flanigan

Birthday   12/20/1935

Carol is a friend of my mom's and we got to know each other on a bowling league. Wow, that seems like years ago - oh wait, it was. We get together with our bowling team about 9 times a year for lunch, but no more bowling involved... Carol lives in Greenwood, IN near her kids and grandkids. It is always fun to hear the stories of her life adventures.

Eileen Tucker

Eileen is married to Granny' son Scott. We have had a special friendship through the years that is hard to describe. We have been with each other through some very tough times of our lives and I will never forget what a great friend she is. We don't stay in touch well today, but when we do see each other we always pick up where we left off - and those are some long lunches because we have a lot of catching up to do.
She spends hours of time in the kitchen creating new dishes and is a cook now for a girls sorority at UC. I am waiting for her cookbook to come out.
She has three girls, Laura, Beth and Hannah plus rescues strays in the neighborhood and sometimes all the way from Florida.

Ellen Dodd

Birthday   7/14/1947

Ellen came into my life thru the Bright Vet Clinic over 20 years ago. She has enriched my life in many ways. Not only is she a great cook (that's why her recipes are in my book), but she collects strays like me. Most of her strays are cats. She has increased my knowledge of the feline ten fold. We collect quite a few other things also (Baskets, Vera Bradley etc), but I won't go into that now. We are both OCD and I am proud to call her a dear friend.

Biographies

Grandma Schilling

Birthday   9/25/1927

Grandma Schilling was another "great cook". She did so much with so little. In another life, when I was married, she taught me a lot about cooking with what you had available. Her Thanksgiving dinners were always yummy!!

Granny Tucker

Birthday   4/17/1932

Dorothy and John attended church with Little Grammy and Joe. Over the years we began to call them Granny and Papa because we were so close and my kids were the only "grandkids" at the time. Granny and Papa were incredible people and ones I am so proud to have as friends. Next to Little Grammy, Granny is the best cook I will ever know.

They have two children, Scott and Lynn who in time gave them 5 grandchildren and one great grand child. Granny lives in Milford today with her dog, Josh. Papa passed away several years ago and is greatly missed.

Holly Schilling

Birthday   9/2/1969

Holly is married to Frank, my children's cousin. She has three young boys and spends lots of time scrapbooking and doing Longaberger with Becki. Holly took care of Aunt Flo at the end and kept her comfortable, for that I will always be grateful.

Jane Strasser

Birthday   7/7/1963

Dr. Jane (a VP at UC) is one of the two people who has made Red Wolf Sanctuary what it is today. The animals are her priority. She has so enriched my life. I am glad to call her a friend. She's also a great traveling companion.

Julie Schilling

Birthday   11/22/1978

Julie came into my life when she met and married my youngest son, Aaron. I can't tell you how blessed I feel with Julie as my daughter-in-law and mother to Esther and Glory. My son has excellent taste. She cooks, sews, teaches, and makes a wonderful home. I look forward to many more years of enjoying & loving Aaron, Julie, Esther and Glory.

Kathy Jones Kinslow

Birthday   3/18/1949

Kathy grew up in Sayler Park also. She was another one of my canasta buddies as kids and we played together for years until she moved to Tennessee. I don't get to see her much anymore, but Bev keeps me updated. After the tornado in April of 74 she took Brian who was 18 months and kept him for several days while we were trying to get settled at Little Grammy and Joe's.

Katie Noppert

Birthday   5/30/1925

I grew up just a few doors down the

street from Katie and her family. We lived there until the tornado of 1974 and Katie still lives in the same house today. I don't ever remember not knowing her. My mom, Ellen, Katie and I play cards once a month and the stakes are high - I always have to buy nickels. Before cards, we do lunch and the recipes from Katie have made a great meal.

Kay Kolb

In 1971 we moved in next door to the Kolb's, while we only lived there for 3 years they made quite an impact on my life. I am so thankful to have been neighbors with such a great couple. Kay has so much talent - not only did she make my favorite cookies ever, but she could sew anything. I still cherish a Christmas tree skirt that she made for me and my daughter still has a doll that she made for her. She is such a delightful person.

Kim Craig

Birthday   8/14/1963

Believe it or not I met Kim in 1986 when she started doing my hair. Now you know why I never have gray hair. After all this time, I am proud to call Kim a friend. Every year at Christmas she brings me a huge platter of yummy cookies. They are all in this book.

Little Grammy

Birthday   11/1/1886

Little Grammy (Elizabeth Fowler) was

my mom's mom. She married Joseph Burger on June 13, 1913 at the age of 26 - he was only 23, but turned 24 the next day. Joe, as we called him to the frustration of Little Grammy, was born on what became Flag Day in 1916. Little Grammy and Joe had two daughters and adopted their first grandchild.

Little Grammy was born in Kentucky and her father, William Fowler had several slaves. The adjustment of not having slaves after the Civil War was hard. Instead of getting up to put another log on the fire, he would just move his chair closer to the stove. Little Grammy had two sisters and one brother, plus a set of twins that died.

Little Grammy was a volunteer at Red Cross for over 65 years. She was not only the best cook I ever knew, but she could sew, embroider, crochet, quilt, cross stitch, and needlepoint. She was never much for housecleaning - must be heredity. She was a very progressive woman for that time period; had she been born in this century she would have achieved even greater heights.

Marshann Kinman

Birthday   3/20/1973

I just met Marshann this year (2009). She worked at the tax office with me. Marsh was always willing to lend a helping hand and learn everything she could to help. She also made yummy apple cinnamon bars. Be sure and try them. Hint - she says the only place she can find the cinnamon chips is at

Biographies

"Biggs".

Mike Padenich

Birthday   9/13/1972

I'm not really sure when I got to know Mike. My son and son-in-law both went to college and had a fraternity brother named Jeffrey Mickey. All of these "boys" are into racing. Jeff lives near Cleveland. When he comes down for races, he brings Mike along. So since 1997 we have seen Mike twice a year during the Indy 500 and the Brickyard. He has become a very important part of all of our lives. When he's here he plays with the dogs and cats and relaxes. It's a win-win for both of us.

Mom

Birthday   7/14/1929

Mom (Nancy Burger Ziegler) was the second daughter of Little Grammy and Joe. Little Grammy was 44 years old when Mom was born (no fertility needed then). Mom grew up in Sayler Park her whole life; not moving until the tornado of 1974. My dad (Dale L Ziegler) grew up there also and they were married on April 22, 1947 while he was on leave from the Army. They have 3 children - I have an older and younger brother and really played the only girl card a lot (worked better with Dad). After 62 years of marriage - I look forward to celebrating their 70th and then 75th anniversaries.

Pam Elliott

Birthday   3/18/1956

Pam came into my life with her partner Jeane thru real estate and mortgages. They are so much fun to be around. Jeane gives my dogs manicures and pedicures and Pam helps with cooking whenever needed. We all try and get together once a month for dinner. It's always a great time. They have both enhanced my life.

Sara Eiding Kassow

Birthday   3/20/1978

Sara is Bev's daughter. She has moved around a lot because her husband is in the Navy but we love to visit with her when she is able to come home for a trip. She is just as sweet as her mother and we share a bond on how we feed our dogs. She also taught me about Keifer.

Sheila Byrd

Sheila and her husband Benny take care of my parents and help them out with almost everything. They are some of the best "people" that I know. They also help keep all my outdoor furniture looking new at my house. I can't imagine what life would be like without them.

Stacey Pruitt

Birthday   7/5/1974

I met Stacey many years ago when she and my son Brian were in high school together. Sometimes high school romances don't work out, but Stacey has always had a special place in my heart. Maybe her being with Brian was how the two of us were to get to know each other and I am glad we did. We have vacationed together and I just enjoy her company.

Special thanks also for re-reading my cookbook. After Jeane finished proofing the book - I added more recipes and bios.

Suzanne Horn

Birthday   4/28/1970

Suzanne and Greg live next door to me, we both moved here about the same time. She's always got whatever it is I need to for cooking that I "forgot" or ran out of. The Horns give out the best Halloween candy in the neighborhood. They have been good neighbors to have.